SEM   CHILDREN 92 STEWART
   2010
Orr, Tamra
Kristen Stewart

Seminary   09/14/2009

SEMINARY SOUTH BRANCH

Blue Banner Biography

Kristen Stewart

Tamra Orr

Mitchell Lane

PUBLISHERS

P.O. Box 196
Hockessin, Delaware 19707
Visit us on the web: www.mitchelllane.com
Comments? email us: mitchelllane@mitchelllane.com

Mitchell Lane
PUBLISHERS

Printing   1   2   3   4   5   6   7   8   9

Blue Banner Biographies

Akon
Allen Iverson
Ashton Kutcher
Beyoncé
Britney Spears
Chris Daughtry
Ciara
Condoleezza Rice
David Ortiz
Eve
Gwen Stefani
Ja Rule
Jessica Simpson
John Legend
Justin Berfield
Kate Hudson
Kenny Chesney
Leona Lewis
Mariah Carey
Mary-Kate and Ashley Olsen
Nancy Pelosi
Orlando Bloom
Peyton Manning
Rihanna
Sally Field
Shakira
Taylor Swift
Tim McGraw
Vanessa Anne Hudgens

Alan Jackson
Ashanti
Avril Lavigne
Bow Wow
Carrie Underwood
Christina Aguilera
Clay Aiken
Corbin Bleu
Derek Jeter
Fergie (Stacy Ferguson)
Ice Cube
Jay-Z
J. K. Rowling
Johnny Depp
Justin Timberlake
Keith Urban
Kristen Stewart
Lil Wayne
Mario
Miguel Tejada
Natasha Bedingfield
P. Diddy
Pink
Ron Howard
Sean Kingston
Shontelle Layne
T.I.
Toby Keith
Zac Efron

Alicia Keys
Ashlee Simpson
Bernie Mac
Brett Favre
Chris Brown
Christopher Paul Curtis
Cole Hamels
Daniel Radcliffe
Eminem
50 Cent
Jamie Foxx
Jennifer Lopez
Joe Flacco
JoJo
Kanye West
Kelly Clarkson
Lance Armstrong
Lindsay Lohan
Mary J. Blige
Missy Elliott
Nelly
Paris Hilton
Queen Latifah
Rudy Giuliani
Selena
Soulja Boy Tell 'Em
Timbaland
Usher

Library of Congress Cataloging-in-Publication Data
Orr, Tamra.
  Kristen Stewart / by Tamra Orr.
     p. cm. — (Blue banner biographies)
  Includes bibliographical references and index.
  ISBN 978-1-58415-773-1 (library bound)
  1. Stewart, Kristen, 1990– —Juvenile literature. 2. Actors—United States—Biography—Juvenile literature. I. Title.
  PN2287.S685O77 2009
  791.4302'8092—dc22
  [B]
                                                                                      2009006309

ABOUT THE AUTHOR: Tamra Orr is the author of more than 200 books for young people and families, including Mitchell Lane's biographies on Jordin Sparks, Brenda Song, and Orlando Bloom. A former English teacher, she lives in the Pacific Northwest, where she alternates between her research and looking at the mountains. Orr's books have won several national awards.

PUBLISHER'S NOTE: The following story has been thoroughly researched, and to the best of our knowledge represents a true story. While every possible effort has been made to ensure accuracy, the publisher will not assume liability for damages caused by inaccuracies in the data and makes no warranty on the accuracy of the information contained herein. This story has not been authorized or endorsed by Kristen Stewart.

Blue Banner Biography

Kristen Stewart's face is a familiar one—from movies, magazines, and the Internet. Not only is she a superstar in the film world, but she is also an icon for popular fashion styles.

Accidental Discovery

When Kristen Stewart walked out on the stage of California elementary school, she was focusing on her lines. She did not realize that her performance would change her life. But it would! Like most kids in her school, eight-year-old Stewart had a part in the annual Christmas show. As she stood on stage and sang, she had no clue that a talent agent was in the audience listening to the performances. He spotted something in her that appealed to him. It was not that she had the perfect voice or was more attractive than any of the other students. There was simply "something" about her that told him she had potential for bigger and better things.

Although many children would be shocked and thrilled to find out that they had a chance to be in movies or on television, Stewart took the news in stride. Many others were not surprised, either. Her acting talent was most likely in her genes—or at least picked up through her daily life. After all, her father, John Stewart, was a stage manager who produced and directed a number of shows for the Fox television network, and her Australian mother, Jules Mann-Stewart, was a script supervisor who had already worked on such

It may be hard to glimpse the future star of blockbuster movies in this young tomboy, but, by 2002, the year this photo was taken, Kristen was already appearing in multiple films and television shows. Unlike those of many other young actors, Stewart's roles were usually serious ones.

films as *Mortal Kombat*, *Flubber*, and *The Phantom*, plus television series such as *Picket Fences* and *The Practice*. Being part of the Hollywood world was quite familiar to Kristen from as early as she can remember. As she puts it, she "fell into acting."

Soon, Stewart, nicknamed KStew by her growing number of fans, began trying out for roles—but not the typical kid roles. "I was vehemently turned away from all of the kiddie auditions," she explains. "I never got any commercials or anything on the Disney Channel. I was always much too serious." Despite this apparent exclusion, Stewart's first role was a non-speaking one in Disney's television movie *The Thirteenth Year*. Stewart was just nine years old at the time.

Over the next decade, Stewart kept working. She appeared in eighteen films in that short period of time. Although her performance in each one was well done, it was as the vampire-loving Bella Swan in the movie *Twilight* that would make the world aware of this young actress, who just happened to "fall" into acting.

> "I never got any commercials or anything on the Disney Channel. I was always much too serious."

Stewart and Jodie Foster hunker down in **Panic Room.** *One of Stewart's best reviewed roles was as Foster's daughter. Her ability to play a diabetic girl being threatened by burglars and her health was powerful.*

A Career Begins

Born on April 9, 1990, in Woodland Hills, California, Kristen Jaymes Stewart almost seemed destined to become an actress. Growing up in Los Angeles, with her parents both involved in creating movies and television shows, guided her to a career in front of the camera. "I grew up on a set," she says. "I don't take [acting] as seriously, and then, at the same time, I take it more seriously than anyone. It's like a balance."

After her brief role on *The Thirteenth Year*, Stewart was hired to play Sam Jennings, daughter of newly divorced Annette (Patricia Clarkson) in *The Safety of Objects*. Not long after that, she got the "big break" that so many young actors hope for. She was cast as Sarah Altman, the diabetic daughter of single mom Meg Altman (Jodie Foster), in the 2002 film *Panic Room*. Hayden Panettiere, a star in the television show *Heroes*, was originally cast in the part but had to be replaced.

In *Panic Room*, burglars break into the Altmans' new home, and the mother and daughter hide in the home's secret room. It is a very suspenseful and sometimes violent movie. Sarah's role called for Stewart not only to act very frightened, but also to physically suffer from complications of her diabetes.

When she realized that she was going to work with Jodie Foster, Stewart was shocked. "I was kind of freaked out at first," she admits. "[Jodie] is not just an actress, she's not one-dimensional. She has more than one creative outlet. She's a writer, producer, a director. She has a pretty level head on her shoulders. . . . I admire most of her values. She's pretty cool." In an article in *Elle*, Foster also commented on her costar. "Her approach is very different from most actors," she said. "She's stoic. She keeps it all wrapped up."

> "Her approach is very different from most actors," Jodie Foster said. "She's stoic. She keeps it all wrapped up."

When the movie was released, critics praised the acting ability of the twelve-year-old Stewart. *Panic Room* made more than $30 million in its opening weekend, and Stewart was nominated for best lead actress at the Young Artist Awards. It changed her life—but not necessarily in positive ways. "It was terrible," she recalls. "I hated going back to school. I did *Panic Room* when I was in the sixth grade. Even though it was just one movie and wasn't a big deal, people would come up and scream at me in the halls. People were actually mean. . . . I got all this attention and so I just changed schools. I thought it was people who I'd grown up with just being rude, but it still continued." She adds, "Kids are mean. It was terrible." From that point on, Stewart stopped going to public school and instead enrolled in correspondence schools. In interviews, she has stated that she

In Cold Creek Manor, *Stewart shared the screen with well-known stars. Once again, she showed audiences that she knew how to play an intense and suspenseful role even though she was still quite young.*

does not miss going to traditional school at all. "I still have my really close friends. I still have my family. I'm really family-oriented, so no, I don't have a problem with it all."

The next film for Stewart was a creepy mystery called *Cold Creek Manor*, with costars Dennis Quaid and Sharon Stone. It was not a big hit, but she soon landed another role in a family film, *Catch That Kid*. In this movie, she plays Maddy, one of three kids who are trying to break into a bank to steal $250,000 so that they can help Maddy's father get an important operation. It was the first movie in which Stewart was considered the lead, or main character.

Even though Stewart was only fifteen, she had already starred in more than half a dozen movies. Her biggest roles were still to come.

In 2004, Stewart was in an emotional Showtime picture called *Speak*. She plays a young girl who has been traumatized so badly that she stops talking. The same year, she was cast in *Zathura: A Space Adventure*, a movie based on a book by Chris Van Allsburg, the author of another popular book/movie combination, *Jumanji*. Stewart plays Lisa, the older sister of two mischievous brothers who find that they are in way over their heads when playing a board game results in having their house flung out into space.

For a good portion of the movie, Stewart is frozen (since she is put into suspended animation). An entire body cast was made of her for the role, and having it made was a very strange experience for her. "It's an experience that no human being has ever really done unless they have a twin; standing next to themselves," she comments. "It also doesn't really help that she's frozen and her lips are blue and her hair is all frosted. I did have to stand pretty still when they were molding the cast." According to Stewart, creating the cast was a complicated, three-step process. First, her body was digitally scanned by a computer, and then each part of her body was molded. It was not necessarily much fun—especially when the head was cast. "I'm pretty claustrophobic and . . . the plaster is warm, so you can't even feel the air go into your

Stewart's body cast looked remarkably lifelike. Her brothers, actors Josh Hutcherson (left) and Jonah Bobo (right), were certainly fooled.

nose because it's warm," she explains. "I mean, you're breathing but it's kind of scary."

Zathura had quite a few special effects in it, but much of what happened was real. "When we harpooned walls and ripped them out, we were really doing it," she admits. "When there was a fire on the set, there was really fire. . . . I got to wear a harness and fly up to the rafters of the sound stage. . . . It was awesome."

Even though Stewart was only fifteen, she had already starred in more than half a dozen movies. Her biggest roles were still to come.

In **The Messengers**, *Stewart plays a character who is frightened most of the time. She perfected the scared look in scene after scene.*

Becoming "That Girl" in the Movie

Slowly but steadily, Kristen Stewart was becoming well known. When she starred in a supernatural horror movie called *The Messengers* in 2007, her image was put on the cover of *Teen Vogue* magazine. "Sometimes people come up to me and ask, 'Are you that girl from that movie?' and I say no," she states. "I guess that's probably going to get a lot harder to get away with."

In *The Messengers*, a family moves out to a farm to get away from hectic city life. Naturally, they move into a spooky old house, and the only one who is able to see the danger is Stewart's character, Jess—but of course, no one believes her. "I'm catatonically terrified in [the movie] most of the time," Stewart recalls. She says the movie was set out in the middle of nowhere and that Jess is alone most of the time. "Towards the end, she basically has to suck it up and figure out why this is happening and get to the bottom of it." The film also stars Dylan McDermott, Penelope Ann Miller, and John Corbett.

That year was busy for Stewart. After *The Messengers*, she starred in *In the Land of Women* and *Into the Wild*. Stewart

Stewart's looks are constantly changing, including her shift to blond hair after filming *Into the Wild*. *It was another step in her growing-up process, as she changed from girl to young woman.*

described *In the Land of Women* as a "drama/comedy." In it, she plays Lucy, an anxious, rebellious teenager and daughter to Sarah, played by actress Meg Ryan. Adam Brody, JoBeth Williams, and Olympia Dukakis are also in the movie. "Lucy is a very inward person," Stewart says about her character. "[She] is like so many of my friends, so many girls I know. She's kind of grooving along being herself then all of a sudden, she's like the popular girl and all that attention kind of freaks her out. She doesn't know how to deal with that, plus she's got this complicated relationship with her mother that holds a lot of resentment."

Stewart's role as Tracy in *Into the Wild*, based on Jon Krakauer's bestselling nonfiction book, was one of her favorites. The film focuses on the story of Christopher McCandless (played by Emile Hirsch), who graduated from college, gave away all his money and possessions, and then hitchhiked to Alaska so that he could live in the wilderness. The film was written and directed by Sean Penn and stars veteran actors William Hurt, Hal Holbrook, and Marcia Gay Harden.

In the film, Tracy is an innocent, hippie-like girl living in Slab City, an RV camp in the California desert. McCandless stops by the camp during his travels. Slab City attracts all kinds of people, and Stewart is fascinated by Tracy's character. "She lives in this place that is totally about people who've gotten away from society, who are sort of like Chris, yet they are still rooted in one place," she describes. "But when Tracy meets Chris, she just falls for him. He has such a love for life. All she wants to do is be with him. Of course, one of the things about Chris is that he didn't really have girlfriends or anything like that. It just wasn't something that mattered to him."

"I sort of follow from here [pointing to her heart]. That's sort of what leads me and the same with them," Kristen said of her character in *Into the Wild.*

At the audition for Penn, Stewart won the role when she played the song "Blackbird" on her guitar. "[Blackbird is] a hard song to sing to. I'm not a singer," she states. Later, she had to play and sing in the movie, in front of a large crowd. "I've never played music for anyone," she says. "But they

At the Los Angeles premiere of Into the Wild, *Stewart arrived with her costars Vince Vaughn and Emile Hirsch. Her role in the film was one of her favorites.*

were a really warm crowd — they were clapping and stoked to be there. That made it a lot of fun."

One of the reasons that Stewart liked playing Tracy was because she recognized quite a bit of herself in the character and related to her lifestyle. "Those people don't really live very differently from the way we do or I do," she explains. "They are just away. I sort of follow from here [pointing to her heart]. That's sort of what leads me and the same with them. I don't feel like I need to get away from something. I've always been given as much freedom as I need so it's not something that I fight for, but, under different circumstances, I have that spirit in me."

Yet Another Adventure

Perhaps because KStew was raised in Los Angeles and surrounded by actors, scripts, and cameras, the job of acting is just that to her—a job. When asked which role she has liked best so far, she replies, "They feel the same to me. . . . Well, the press is different, but the making of the films is always the same for me."

In 2008, she landed another unusual role, this time in a film called *Adventureland*. This comedy/drama was written and directed by Greg Mottola, the same person who created the movie *Superbad*. It is based loosely on Mottola's life and is set in an amusement park during the year 1987. Along with Stewart, the cast includes Jesse Eisenberg and Wendie Malick. "Greg's films are so real," says Stewart. "They're about real people, and it's not trying to be anything. He just takes a snippet of somebody's life."

In *Adventureland*, Stewart plays Emily Lewin, a young girl who works at the carnival. Em is based on a "compilation of a couple different girls [Greg] had dated when he was younger. . . . Really sort of complicated, damaged, messed up girls," describes Stewart. An unhappy teen, she is torn

Stewart, along with friends and costars Nikki Reed (left) from Twilight *and Kat Dennings (right) from* Nick and Norah's Infinite Playlist, *spent time together at the L.A. premiere of* Adventureland.

between two men and constantly searching for answers that will make her happy. "She works at the park with these guys," she relates, "and is as miserable as they are, and they can relate to that. She has a really hard time coming out of herself and she—at least for a summer—lets her face hang out for a minute."

Besides playing her part, Stewart also used the experience to help her get over a lifetime phobia. "I was always afraid of Disney Land," she says with a chuckle. "Because there was an urban legend that they used to steal the kids and shave their heads. They'd take them out of the parks, and then the park would shut down to try to find the bald child. I never wanted to be that child!"

In between making movies, Stewart has found time to date. Ever since she was fourteen years old, her boyfriend has been actor Michael Angarano. Like Stewart, he is a familiar face from a number of different films, including *Speak* with KStew, *Sky High*, and *The Forbidden Kingdom*. He has also appeared in a variety of television shows, including *Will and Grace*.

For almost ten years, Stewart made films that were praised and criticized, popular and not, but it was her next role that would put her face in countless movie theaters and bookstores across the country. As Bella Swan, the young girl hopelessly in love with vampire Edward Cullen, she would soon be so well recognized that she would need bodyguards and disguises for the first time.

> *She would soon be so well recognized that she would need bodyguards and disguises for the first time.*

As Bella Swan, Stewart became a huge superstar. Her image appeared on posters, bookmarks, T-shirts, calendars, and countless other types of merchandise that tied into the movie.

Twilight and Beyond

When author Stephenie Meyer wrote her first of four books about the passion between vampire Edward Cullen (to be played by Robert Pattinson) and human Bella Swan in 2003, she most likely had no idea that she was about to start a movement that would sweep across the country and create millions of young fans. One person who actually did not read the books was Kristen Stewart. When she was offered the role of Bella in the *Twilight* movie, she did not even know who the character was. "I read a synopsis of the story before I read the script or the book—and hated it," Stewart admitted in November 2008. "I didn't want to be part of something that presents this really ideological idea of love to so many young people." The synopsis apparently painted a picture of Bella that was weak and that annoyed Stewart. Everything changed when she read the actual script, however. "Once I read the script, I begged for an audition," she says. "[Bella] becomes the assertive force in the relationship. It's an ambitious thing to try to portray the ultimate love story, and I thought it would be a good project."

As Stewart got involved in making the *Twilight* movie, she realized how important it was to the readers that the characters were portrayed properly. "I felt such a responsibility to the story first and to the character," she told Steve Weintraub in 2008. "If you don't get to play the part that really compels you then they might die right on the page and no one gets to experience them as you have, and that was much stronger than my ideas about the fans."

When *Twilight* opened in the theaters, it earned $7 million in sales in its first night! All of a sudden, photographs and interviews with its stars were splashed across the covers of magazines, newspapers, and television entertainment channels, as well as movie merchandise such

Millions of Twilight *fans, many of them young women, follow every story and interview about their favorite star, KStew. These fans stood outside the Garden State Plaza in Paramus, New Jersey, for a promotional event for the movie in November 2008.*

The love story between Robert Pattinson's Edward and Stewart's Bella captured the attention of fans all over the country. The film was quickly rated number one in theaters across the nation.

as posters, T-shirts, and calendars. All of this attention helped increase ticket sales, but it has also made the stars, including Stewart, very easy to recognize when they go out. Fans are nice—and appreciated—but they can be overwhelming, too.

"I've only had a couple of occasions where I've had to deal with the craze," says Stewart. "At Comic-Con, we were entirely separated from them and that's how it should be. I know Summit's [Summit Entertainment, the company that produced *Twilight*] trying to promote the frenzy, but I'm going to tell them, 'Yo, you have to protect us from this.' I'll have big bodyguards."

With good reason, Stewart was looking forward to a long and rewarding career. Before she reached twenty years old, she had already accomplished so much, and planned to keep doing so for years to come.

Another time, while the cast was in Rome, it happened again. "I was literally thrown into a van. I was being held by my arms by two big security guys and they were getting pushed over by these fifteen-year-old girls, and they let me go for a second, and I just got enveloped," Stewart recalls. "The bodyguards had to pick me up and shove me into the van. Then, the van started rocking because the barricades had broken down and [the fans] swarmed the car. It was totally scary."

What would Stewart do next? By summer 2009, she already had several other films in the works or finished, including *The Runaways*, a movie in which she portrays 1980s rocker Joan Jett, and *K-11*, a movie with *Twilight* costar Nikki Reed. Of course, she was also planning to stay with the

Meyer blockbusters and would star as Bella once again in the next installment, *Twilight Saga: New Moon*.

Going to college is also a possibility—but a fairly remote one. In fall 2008, Stewart said, "Not now, maybe if I can grow up a little bit. But not yet, I can't. It's just I've had a lot of demands put on me for quite a long time."

Whatever decisions she makes, it is clear that acting will be KStew's main goal. When asked why she chose acting, she replied, "There's really no way to put this. . . . Because I have to. I'm not a performer. I can't do a song or dance for you. I don't like 'entertaining' people, that's not why I do it. Acting is such a personal thing . . . but in terms of creative outlets and expressing yourself, it's just the most extreme version of that that I've ever found. It's like running. It's exertion." She adds, "When you reach that point where you can't go anymore and you stop and you take a breath, it's that same sort of clearing of the mind. And when you get to study something else and understand someone else and completely lose yourself in it, you feel a certain responsibility—or at least I do, because if you don't bring that character to life the right way, then nobody else gets to see them or experience what you did."

For a good part of her life, KStew has been bringing characters to life in her own unique way. Whether she is playing Bella once again, or acting in any of her other future roles, she is sure to entertain. After all, it is in her blood.

"Acting is such a personal thing . . . in terms of creative outlets and expressing yourself . . ."

1990 Kristen Jaymes Stewart is born on April 9 in Woodland Hills, California.

1998 At a school play, she is discovered by a talent agent.

1999 She appears in *The Thirteenth Year*.

2001 She has a role in *The Safety of Objects*.

2002 After the success of *Panic Room*, she withdraws from public school and begins taking correspondence courses.

2004 She is in *Speak*, and begins dating Michael Angarano. She also has roles in *Catch That Kid* and *Undertow*.

2005 She has roles in *Fierce People* and *Zathura: A Space Adventure*.

2007 A busy year for Kristen, she appears in five movies.

2008 Kristen continues to be busy, but in this year's batch of five movies is *Twilight*. The role of Bella Swan will change her life.

2009 Kristen has roles in several movies, including *Twilight Saga: New Moon*, the second movie in the *Twilight* series. She also works on *Welcome to the Rileys*, *K-11*, and *The Runaways*. She appears with Rob Pattinson at the Gewa Project charity concert.

FILMOGRAPHY

2009 *Twilight Saga: New Moon*

2008 *The Yellow Handkerchief*
What Just Happened
Jumper
Twilight
Adventureland

2007 *In the Land of Women*
The Messengers
The Cake Eaters
Into the Wild
Cutlass

2005 *Fierce People*
Zathura: A Space Adventure

2004 *Speak*
Catch That Kid
Undertow

2003 *Cold Creek Manor*

2002 *Panic Room*

2001 *The Safety of Objects*

FURTHER READING

Books

Hurley, Jo. *Kristen Stewart: Bella of the Ball*. New York: Scholastic, 2009.

Meyer, Stephenie. *The Twilight Saga: The Official Guide*. Boston: Little, Brown Young Readers, 2008.

Works Consulted

Barker, Lynn. "Kristen Stewart: *Zathura*." *Teen Hollywood*, November 8, 2005.
http://www.teenhollywood.com/d.asp?r=110761&c=1038&p=1

Carroll, Larry. "Kristen Stewart Hangs On to Her Indie Roots at Sundance." *MTV.com*, January 21, 2009.
http://www.mtv.com/movies/news/articles/1603065/story.jhtml

Dobuzinskis, Alex. "For *Twilight* Star Kristen Stewart, Life Is Just a Big Adventureland." *The Vancouver Sun*, January 31, 2009.
http://www.vancouversun.com/Travel/Twilight+star+Kristen+Stewart+life+just+Adventureland/1237508/story.html

Fanning, Evan. "Kids Have Been So Mean to Me," *Independent.ie*, December 14, 2008.
http://www.independent.ie/entertainment/film-cinema/kids-have-been-so-mean-to-me-1574361.html

In the Land of Women: "Interview Kristen Stewart." *Visual Hollywood*.
http://www.visualhollywood.com/movies/in_land_women/about4.php

Kristen Stewart Biography, *People.com*.
http://www.people.com/people/kristen_stewart

Roberst, Sheila. "Kristen Stewart Interview: *Into the Wild*." *Movies Online*,
http://www.moviesonline.ca/movienews_13017.html

FURTHER READING

"*Twilight* Countdown: Kristen Stewart Talks About Becoming Bella." *L.A. Times*, November 10, 2008.
http://latimesblogs.latimes.com/entertainmentnewsbuzz/2008/11/twilight-coun-8.html

Weintraub, Steve. "Kristen Stewart Interview *Twilight*." *Collider.com*, November 9, 2008.
http://www.collider.com/entertainment/interviews/article.asp?aid=9789&tcid=1

West, Steven. "Sundance Interview: Kristen Stewart and Jesse Eisenberg." *Cinema Blend.com*, January 25, 2009.
http://www.cinemablend.com/new/Sundance-Interview-Kristen-Stewart-And-Jesse-Eisenberg-11729.html

Web Addresses

Kristen Stewart Online
   http://www.kristenstewart.net/

Kristen Stewart Fan
   http://www.kstewartfan.org/

Twilight Series
   http://www.stepheniemeyer.com/twilight_movie.html

INDEX